CICADAS

A TRUE BOOK®

by

Ann O. Squire

Children's Press®

A Division of Scholastic Inc.

New York Toronto London Auckland Sydney
Mexico City New Delhi Hong Kong
Danbury, Connecticut

A cicada's
eyes and
mouthparts

Reading Consultant
Nanci R. Vargus, Ed.D.
Assistant Professor
Literacy Education
University of Indianapolis
Indianapolis, IN

Content Consultant
Alan C. York
Department of Entomology
Purdue University
West Lafayette, IN

Dedication:
For Evan

*The photo on the cover shows
a cicada perched on a leaf. The
photo on the title page shows
a periodical cicada.*

Library of Congress Cataloging-in-Publication Data

Squire, Ann.
   Cicadas / by Ann O. Squire
     p.cm. — (True books)
   Includes bibliographic references and index (p.).
   Contents: The singers of summer—The strange life of a cicada—
Cicada song—Cicada enemies—Cicada mysteries.
   ISBN 0-516-22782-3 (lib. bdg.)   0-516-27766-9 (pbk.)
   1. Cicadas—Juvenile literature. [1. Cicadas.] I. Title. II. True book.
QL527.C5 S69 2003
595.7'52—dc21   200201112

CHILDREN'S PRESS, and A TRUE BOOK®, and associated logos are
trademarks and or registered trademarks of Scholastic Library Publishing.
SCHOLASTIC and associated logos are trademarks and or registered
trademarks of Scholastic Inc.

1 2 3 4 5 6 7 8 9 10 R 12 11 10 09 08 07 06 05 04 03

Contents

You may have spotted a cicada sitting on a tree trunk during the summer.

The Singers of Summer

Have you ever been in your backyard on a summer day and heard a loud buzzing noise coming from the trees? Or have you ever seen something that looks like a huge insect clinging to a tree trunk, but it was actually just an empty shell? If so, you already know a bit about cicadas. These gigantic insects emerge by the thousands during the summer and spend several weeks searching for mates, mating, and laying eggs. Male cicadas are known for their loud, buzzing calls, which are very effective for attracting females (and perhaps also for driving away predators). Cicadas have the reputation of being the noisiest animals in the world,

A male cicada will sing to attract a female.

and when a large group of males sings in unison, the result is surprisingly loud.

Cicadas are also famous for their long life spans.

But as you'll read in the next chapter, a cicada spends most of its life as a **nymph** (an immature cicada). After becoming an adult, a cicada lives for only a few weeks.

A cicada will not live very long as an adult.

Grasshoppers may look like cicadas, but they are not closely related.

Because of their large size and loud songs, adult cicadas are often mistaken for grasshoppers. Despite these similarities, cicadas are not closely related to grasshoppers. It might surprise you to learn that some of the cicada's nearest relatives are tiny green aphids. These little insects harm garden plants by piercing their stems and sucking out the plants' juices.

Like their smaller aphid relatives, cicadas have mouthparts specialized for piercing and sucking. But because they live above the

Although they are much smaller in size, aphids are closely related to cicadas.

ground for only a few weeks, and spend most of that time mating, adult cicadas usually do not harm plants very much.

The Strange Life of a Cicada

Of all the insects in the world, few have life cycles as odd as that of the cicada. These insects have some of the longest life spans in the insect world—up to seventeen years! You might wonder how this can be, since cicadas only

Cicadas have very long life spans.

seem to appear for a few weeks during the summer. Where are they the rest of the time?

Once buzzing male cicadas have found mates, they soon

Male cicadas die soon after mating.

die, and the females prepare to lay their eggs. After choosing a thin twig, the female cuts a small slit in it and lays her eggs inside. After several weeks, the eggs hatch into tiny, wingless nymphs that fall to the ground and immediately dig into the soil, where they suck the sap from tree roots. The nymphs stay underground for years, **molting**

Nymphs molt their exoskeletons frequently as they grow.

(shedding their hard, outer shells called **exoskeletons**) from time to time and growing very slowly. Different types of cicadas spend different amounts of time as nymphs. Some cicadas become adults after two to five years, while others spend either thirteen or seventeen years underground.

Finally, the time comes for the cicadas to leave their underground homes. During the night, the nymphs dig

Cicadas dig themselves out of the ground at night.

their way out of the soil and climb onto the nearest vertical surface, usually a tree trunk. There they molt for the final

After emerging from underground, a cicada will molt one last time.

time, leaving their empty exoskeletons behind.

Once they reach adulthood, cicadas live for only about a month, which is just long enough to mate and lay eggs.

Cicada Invasion

Some areas of the United States are home to thirteen-year and seventeen-year cicadas. Every 221 years, their cycles coincide and they emerge from the ground at the same time. When this happened in Missouri in 1998, some areas were overrun by millions of cicadas per square mile. An event like this won't happen again in Missouri until the year 2219!

Many cicadas may emerge at the same time.

Sometimes cicadas seem to be everywhere!

Cicada Song

Cicadas are best known for their loud, buzzing songs, which fill the air on summer days. To make noise, a cicada uses two drum-like organs on its abdomen, called **tymbals**. The tymbals are connected to strong muscles. When the cicada tightens these muscles,

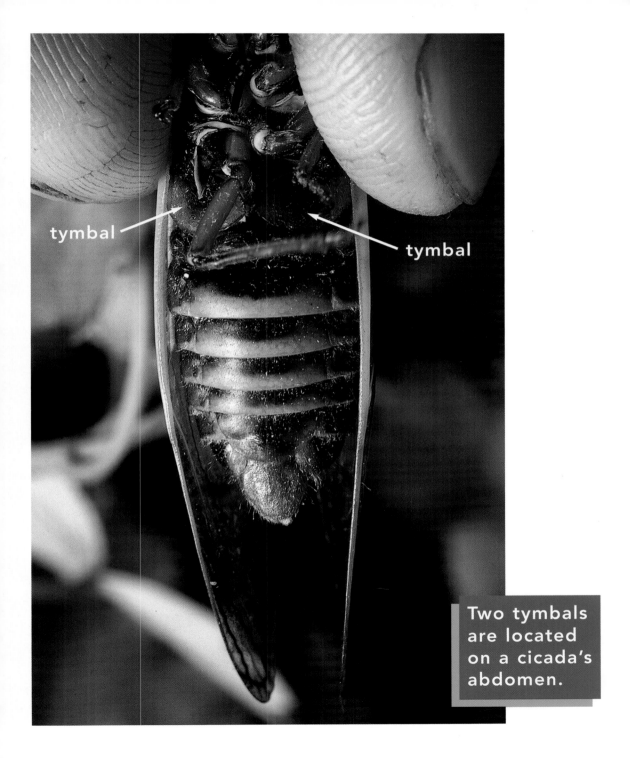

tymbal

tymbal

Two tymbals are located on a cicada's abdomen.

the tymbals bend inward, producing a sound. When the muscles relax, the tymbals pop back into their original positions. The song is created as the cicada tightens and releases the tymbal muscles over and over again.

Although they may all sound the same to you, different kinds of cicadas have their own calls. Only males produce sound, but both male and female cicadas can hear

Each species of cicada
has its own call.

them through large, mirrorlike
membranes called **tympana**.
Female cicadas can hear even
the smallest variations in a
song and will only respond to

A female will find a male of the same species by listening for its call.

a male of their **species**—a group of animals that are alike in important ways. The ability to hear these differences comes in very handy when two or more species of cicadas live in the same area, because it prevents females from mating with males of the wrong species.

Even if you can't tell the difference between the songs of different cicadas, you can't miss the fact that they are

Large cicadas can
make very loud
buzzing noises.

loud, sometimes even painfully loud. Some large cicadas produce sounds louder than 120 **decibels**—about the same as a rock concert or a jackhammer at close range. To avoid going deaf from his own singing, the male cicada has a special trick. When he sings, he folds his tympana so they won't be as sensitive to the sounds he is making.

Cicada Enemies

Even though they are adults for only a few weeks, cicadas face plenty of dangers. Their biggest enemies are birds, which swoop down and pluck them from the trees. They are also eaten by many other **predators**, including dogs and cats, who find

Owls enjoy eating cicadas.

them a tasty summertime treat.

There is even a type of wasp that preys on cicadas.

Giant cicada killers use cicadas to feed their young wasps.

Known as the "giant cicada killer," this large wasp stings its victim with a poison that paralyzes it. Then the wasp carries it back to the nest. The wasp then lays an egg on top of the living but paralyzed cicada. After the egg hatches, the cicada's body serves as food for the developing wasp.

When a cicada is disturbed or threatened, it makes a loud squawking noise. Because this insect does not bite or sting, this alarm call is its only defense, other than flying away. Sometimes the noise is

Cicadas usually fly away when they sense danger.

enough to scare the attacker off or to confuse it long enough for the cicada to escape. If not, the cicada is out of luck.

Because they have so many enemies and so few ways of defending themselves, you

Large cicada populations help to keep the insects from being wiped out by enemies.

With so many cicadas emerging at one time, some are bound to survive.

might think the cicada population would be wiped out after one summer. Fortunately for cicadas, this never happens. Scientists think that the reason cicadas survive from year to year is that so many of these insects appear at the same time that predators just can't eat all of them. Thousands of cicadas may end up as someone's dinner, but there are always enough survivors left behind to mate and produce more cicadas.

Cicada Mysteries

Scientists have studied cicadas for many years, but there are still some mysteries that remain unsolved. Why do they emerge every seventeen years (or every thirteen years in some species)? How do they manage, after all those years underground, to

Scientists are not sure how cicadas know to come out of the ground all at the same time.

come out at the same time?
Some scientists believe their
long and unusual life cycle
helps them to avoid predators

Soil temperature might
be one reason a cicada
comes out of the ground.

that emerge at more "normal" cycles, such as two, four, or six years.

Scientists have a few ideas to explain how cicadas emerge by the thousands during the same time period. Some think that a part of the cicada's brain works as a kind of clock, counting down the years until it is time for the insect to emerge. Others believe that changes in the soil temperature or in the tree sap that cicada nymphs eat are responsible for letting the insects know the time has come to emerge from the ground.

One interesting discovery is that cicada nymphs do not all grow at the same rate while living underground. Some grow rapidly and wait under-ground for as long as a year before emerging as adults. Others grow more slowly and tunnel to the surface as soon

Some cicada nymphs develop slowly underground.

as they reach full size. Despite these differences, they all manage to dig their way out at about the same time.

These nymphs are shedding their last exoskeletons as they reach the top of the soil.

Eventually, scientists may discover the signal that tells cicadas it's time to emerge. Until then, this insect's unusual life cycle will remain one of the mysteries of nature.

Cicadas in China

The Chinese believed cicadas came to life as they crawled out of the ground.

Because of the cicada's ability to emerge from the ground and "come to life," these insects were worshipped in ancient China. It was common to place a carved stone in the shape of a cicada on the tongue of a dead person in the hope that the cicada would magically bring the person back to life.

Cicadas were very important in Chinese culture.

To Find Out More

If you'd like to learn more about cicadas, check out these additional resources.

 **Books**

Anderson, Margret. **Bizarre Insects** (Weird and Wacky Science). New York: Enslow Publishers, 1996.

Clyne, Dennis. **Cicada Sing-Song** (Nature Close-Ups). New York: Gareth Stevens, 2001.

Miller, Sara Swan. **Cicadas and Aphids: What They Have in Common** (Animals in Order). Danbury, CT: Franklin Watts, 1999.

Organizations and Online Sites

Entomology for Kids

*http://www.uky.edu/
agriculture/entomology/
ythfacts/bugfun/bugfun.htm*

Learn more about studying
and collecting insects in
your backyard.

University of Michigan

*http://insects.ummz.lsa.
umich.edu/fauna/
michigan_cicadas*

The University of Michigan
maintains this cicada Web
site. It combines lots of
information, photos, and a
chart of when and where
cicadas are expected to
emerge around the
United States.

Important Words

decibel a measurement of the relative loudness of a sound. The decibel scale runs from zero decibels (db) for the softest sound to 130 db for sound that causes pain.

exoskeleton the hard outer covering of an insect's body

molt to shed an old, outgrown exoskeleton

nymph the immature form of a cicada

predator an animal that hunts, kills, and eats other animals in order to survive

species a group of animals or plants that are of the same kind and that are alike in all important ways

tymbal a drum-like organ that the cicada uses to produce sound

tympana vibrating membranes that serve as the cicada's hearing organs

Index

Meet the Author

Ann O. Squire has a Ph.D. in animal behavior. Before becoming a writer, she spent several years studying African electric fish and the special signals they use to communicate with each other. Dr. Squire is the author of many books on animals and natural science topics, including *Termites*, *Spiders*, *Ants*, and *Crickets and Grasshoppers*. She lives with her children, Evan and Emma, in Katonah, New York.